U.S. DEPARTMENT OF LABOR   Occupational Safety and Health Administration

DIRECTIVE NUMBER: CPL 02-01-051   **EFFECTIVE DATE:** May 20, 2011

SUBJECT: 29 CFR Part 1915, Subpart B, Confined and Enclosed Spaces and Other Dangerous Atmospheres in Shipyard Employment

ABSTRACT

Purpose: This instruction provides current policy, inspection procedures, information and guidance to ensure uniform enforcement of the 29 CFR Part 1915, Subpart B standard which became effective on October 24, 1994.

Scope: OSHA-wide.

References: See paragraph V.

Cancellation: OSHA Instruction CPL 02-01-042, September 7, 2005.

State Impact: State notice of intent and equivalency required (see paragraph VII.).

Action Offices: National, Regional, and Area Offices.

Originating Office: Directorate of Enforcement Programs.

Contact: Director, Office of Maritime Enforcement
200 Constitution Avenue, N.W., Room N-3610
Washington, D.C. 20210
(202) 693-2399

By and Under the Authority of

David Michaels, PhD, MPH
Assistant Secretary

Executive Summary

This instruction provides guidance to Occupational Safety and Health Administration (OSHA) national, regional, and area offices; industry employer and employee groups; and State programs and federal agencies concerning OSHA's policy and procedures for implementing intervention and inspection programs to reduce or eliminate workplace hazards related to confined and enclosed spaces and other dangerous atmospheres in shipyard employment. As detailed in the Department of Labor's Strategic Plan, OSHA is particularly committed to focused interventions to reduce injuries, illnesses and fatalities in all industries, including shipyard employment.

This instruction provides information and guidance to support intervention and inspection programs related to shipyard employment. This instruction:

- Supports DOL's Strategic Plan for increased emphasis on improving occupational safety and health in all industries, including shipyard employment.

- Provides OSHA compliance officers and consultants and other interested government and industry parties with information to support confined and enclosed spaces and other dangerous atmospheres intervention efforts and to minimize employee exposure to hazards.

- Supports the Site-Specific Targeting (SST) program for the shipbuilding and ship repairing industries, and the National Emphasis Program (NEP) on Shipbreaking.

Significant Changes

This instruction has been revised and updated to include significant changes as follows:

- Updates references and directives to include new documents and the current version of documents previously listed.

- Delivers available shipyard employment safety and health information in a web-based format with additional electronic links to noted references.

- Includes six flowcharts in Appendix A for easy reference. These flowcharts were previously developed and posted on OSHA's website to clarify the logical process for determining compliance with 29 CFR Part 1915, Subpart B requirements.

- Revises the format of the instruction to comply with current Agency procedures.

Table of Contents

I.   Purpose. This instruction provides national, regional, and area offices with guidance concerning OSHA's policy and procedures on the enforcement of safety and health standards for confined and enclosed spaces and other dangerous atmospheres in shipyard employment (i.e., ship repair, shipbuilding, and shipbreaking). In support of DOL's Strategic Plan, OSHA is particularly committed to focused interventions in shipyard employment to reduce injuries, illnesses and fatalities.

II.   Scope. This instruction applies OSHA-wide to all intervention and inspection programs involving confined and enclosed spaces and other dangerous atmospheres in shipyard employment.

III. Cancellation. This instruction cancels the following:

OSHA Instruction CPL 02-01-042, *29 CFR Part 1915, Subpart B, Confined and Enclosed Spaces and Other Dangerous Atmospheres in Shipyard Employment*, September 7, 2005.

IV.   Significant Changes. This instruction supports confined and enclosed spaces and other dangerous atmospheres intervention and inspection programs in the shipyard employment industry. This instruction has been revised and updated to include significant changes as follows:

- Updates references and directives to include new documents and the current version of documents previously listed.

- Delivers available shipyard employment safety and health information in a web-based format with additional electronic links to noted references.

- Includes six flowcharts in Appendix A for easy reference. These flowcharts were previously developed and posted on OSHA's website to clarify the logical process for determining compliance with 29 CFR Part 1915, Subpart B requirements

- Revises the format of the instruction to comply with current Agency procedures.

V.   References.

A.   29 CFR Part 1910, General Industry Standards.

B.   29 CFR Part 1915, Shipyard Employment Standards.

C.   Department of Labor 2011-2016 Strategic Plan, Department of Labor Strategic Plan for Fiscal Years 2011-2016.

D.   29 CFR Part 1960, Basic Program Elements for Federal Employee Occupational Safety and Health Programs and Related Matters.

E.   Shipyard Employment Safety Standards, Subpart B Final Rule, Federal Register 59:37816 – 59:37863, July 25, 1994.

F.   OSHA Instructions.

      1.   OSHA Notice 10-06 (CPL 02), Site-Specific Targeting 2010 (SST-10), August 18, 2010.

      2.   OSHA Instruction CPL 03-00-012, OSHA's National Emphasis Program (NEP) on Shipbreaking, November 4, 2010.

      3.   OSHA Instruction CPL 02-00-142, Shipyard Employment "Tool Bag" Directive, August 3, 2006.

      4.   OSHA Instruction CPL 02-00-150, OSHA Field Operations Manual (FOM), April 22, 2011.

      5.   OSHA Instruction CPL 02-01-047, OSHA Authority Over Vessels and Facilities on or Adjacent to U.S. Navigable Waters and the Outer Continental Shelf (OCS), February 22, 2010.

      6.   OSHA Instruction CPL 02-01-049, 29 CFR Part 1915, Subpart I, Enforcement Guidance for Personal Protective Equipment (PPE) in Shipyard Employment, November 4, 2010.

      7.   OSHA Instruction CSP 01-03-001, Maritime Jurisdiction in State Plan States, October 30, 1978.

VI.   Expiration Date. This instruction will remain in effect until canceled or superseded by another OSHA Directive.

VII.   Federal Program Change.

This instruction describes a federal program change for which notice of intent and equivalency are required. States with OSHA-approved State Plans that cover private sector shipyard employment activities, as well as those with public sector employees engaged in these activities, are expected to have implementing enforcement policies and procedures in place for their confined spaces, enclosed spaces and other dangerous atmospheres which are at least as effective as those in this instruction. All States with OSHA-approved State Plans cover public sector employees, State and local government employees, including any public employees that may be engaged in maritime activities; only California, Minnesota, Vermont and Washington cover private sector shore-side operations for shipyard employment and marine terminals (see 29 CFR 1952, *Approved State Plans for Enforcement of State Standards*).

States with private or public sector shipyard employees within their jurisdiction are required to notify OSHA within 60 days whether they intend to adopt policies and procedures identical to those in this instruction or adopt or maintain different policies and procedures. States without any private or public sector shipyard employment should so indicate in their response.

If a State adopts or maintains policies and procedures that differ from federal policies and procedures, the State must identify the differences and may either post its policy on its website and provide the link to OSHA or submit an electronic copy to OSHA with information on how the public may obtain a copy. If a State adopts policies and procedures that are identical to federal policies and procedures, the State must provide the date of adoption to OSHA. State adoption must be accomplished within 6 months, with posting or submission of documentation within 60 days of adoption. OSHA will post summary information on the State Plan responses to this instruction on its website.

States were required to adopt standards at least as effective as OSHA's confined spaces, enclosed spaces and other dangerous atmospheres in shipyard employment standards by October 24, 1994 (59 FR 37857, July 25, 1994).

VIII. Action Information.

    A.   Responsible Office. Directorate of Enforcement Programs (DEP), Office of Maritime Enforcement (OME).

    B.   Action Offices. National, Regional, and Area Offices; Consultation Project Managers; State Plan States.

    C.   Information Offices. None.

IX. Actions Required. The policies and procedures set forth in this instruction will remain in effect until canceled by proper authority. OSHA Regional Administrators, Area Directors, and National Office Directors must ensure that the policies and procedures set forth in this instruction are followed.

Regional Administrators also must ensure that State Plan State Designees and Consultation Program Managers in their regions are informed of the requirements of this instruction and encourage the involvement of Consultation Programs in promoting 29 CFR Part 1915, Subpart B safety and health requirements.

X. Federal Agencies. This instruction describes a change that may affect federal agencies. It is the responsibility of the head of each federal agency to establish and maintain an effective and comprehensive safety and health program. Executive Order 12196, Section 1-201 and 29 CFR 1960.16 require federal agencies to adopt policies and procedures necessary to provide a level of protection equivalent to that provided by OSHA standards and regulations.

XI. Definitions.

    A.   *Adjacent Spaces*: Those spaces bordering a subject space in all directions, including all points of contact, corners, diagonals, decks, tank tops, and bulkheads.

    B.   *Certified Industrial Hygienist (CIH)*: An industrial hygienist who is certified by the American Board of Industrial Hygiene.

    C.   *Coast Guard Authorized Person*: An individual who meets the requirements of Appendix B to Subpart B of 29 CFR Part 1915 for tank vessels, passenger vessels, and for cargo and miscellaneous vessels.

D.   *Cold Work*: Any work which does not involve riveting, welding, burning or other fire or spark producing operations.

E.   *Competent Person*: A person who is capable of recognizing and evaluating employee exposure to hazardous substances or to other unsafe conditions and is capable of specifying the necessary protection and precautions to be taken to ensure the safety of employees as required by the particular regulation under the condition to which it applies. The competent person also must meet the additional requirements of 1915.7.

F.   *Confined Space*: A compartment of small size and limited access such as a double bottom tank, cofferdam, or other space which by its small size and confined nature can readily create or aggravate a hazardous exposure.

G.   *Dangerous Atmosphere*: An atmosphere that may expose employees to the risk of death, incapacitation, impairment of ability to self-rescue (i.e., escape unaided from a confined or enclosed space), injury, or acute illness.

H.   *Director*: The Director of the National Institute for Occupational Safety and Health, U.S. Department of Health and Human Services, or designated representative.

I.   *Enclosed Space*: Any space, other than a confined space, which is enclosed by bulkheads and overhead. It includes cargo holds, tanks, quarters, machinery, and boiler spaces.

J.   *Enter with Restrictions*: Denotes a space where entry for work is permitted only if engineering controls, personal protective equipment, clothing, and time limitations are as specified by the Marine Chemist, Certified Industrial Hygienist, or the Shipyard Competent Person.

K.   *Entry*: The action by which a person passes through an opening into a space. Entry includes ensuing work activities in that space and is considered to have occurred as soon as any part of the entrant's body breaks the plane of an opening into the space.

L.   *Hot Work*: Any activity involving riveting, welding, burning or the use of powder-actuated tools or similar fire-producing operations. Grinding, drilling, abrasive blasting, or similar spark-producing operations are also considered hot work except when such operations are isolated physically from any atmosphere containing more than 10 percent of the lower explosive limit of a flammable or combustible substance.

M.   *Immediately Dangerous to Life or Health (IDLH)*: An atmosphere that poses an immediate threat to life or that is likely to result in acute or immediate severe health effects.

N.   *Labeled*: Identified with means of a sign, placard, or other form of written communication, including pictograms, that provides information on the status or condition of the work space to which it is attached.

O.   *Lower Explosive Limit (LEL)*: The minimum concentration of vapor in air below which propagation of a flame does not occur in the presence of an ignition source.

P.   *Marine Chemist*: An individual who possesses a current Marine Chemist Certificate issued by the National Fire Protection Association.

Q.   *Nationally Recognized Testing Laboratory (NRTL)*: An organization recognized by OSHA, in accordance with Appendix A of 29 CFR 1910.7, which tests for safety and lists or labels or accepts equipment and materials that meet all the criteria found in 1910.7(b)(1) through (b)(4)(ii).

R.   *Not Safe for Hot Work*: Denotes a space where hot work may not be performed because the conditions do not meet the criteria for Safe for Hot Work.

S.   *Not Safe for Workers*: Denotes a space where an employee may not enter because the conditions do not meet the criteria for Safe for Workers.

T.   *Oxygen-Deficient Atmosphere*: An atmosphere having an oxygen concentration of less than 19.5 percent by volume.

U.   *Oxygen-Enriched Atmosphere*: An atmosphere that contains 22.0 percent or more oxygen by volume.

V.   *Related Employment*: Any employment performed as an incident to or in conjunction with ship repairing, shipbreaking, or shipbuilding work, including, but not restricted to, inspection, testing, and employment as a watchman.

W.   *Safe for Hot Work*: A space that meets all of the following criteria: (1) The oxygen content of the atmosphere does not exceed 22.0 percent by volume; (2) the concentration of flammable vapors in the atmosphere is less than 10 percent of the lower explosive limit; (3) the residues or materials in the space are not capable of producing a higher concentration than permitted in the above (i.e., (1) and (2)), under existing atmospheric conditions in the presence of hot work and while maintained as directed by the Marine Chemist or competent person; and (4) all adjacent spaces have been cleaned, or inerted, or treated sufficiently to prevent the spread of fire.

X.   *Safe for Workers*: A space that meets the following criteria: (1) The oxygen content of the atmosphere is at least 19.5 percent and below 22.0 percent by volume; (2) the concentration of flammable vapors is below 10 percent of the lower explosive limit (LEL); (3) any toxic materials in the atmosphere associated with cargo, fuel, tank coatings, or inerting media are within permissible concentrations at the time of the inspection; and (4) any residues or materials associated with the work authorized by the Marine Chemist, Certified Industrial Hygienist, or competent person will not produce uncontrolled release of toxic materials under existing atmospheric conditions while maintained as directed.

Y.   *Ship Repair*: Any repair of a vessel including, but not restricted to, alterations, conversions, installations, cleaning, painting, and maintenance work.

Z. *Shipbreaking*: Any breaking down of a vessel's structure to dismantle the vessel, including the removal of gear, equipment, or any component of the vessel. This term is commonly referred to as "ship scrapping" and "ship disposal."

AA. *Shipbuilding*: The construction of a vessel including the installation of machinery and equipment.

BB. *Shipyard Employment*: This includes ship repairing, shipbuilding, shipbreaking, and related employments.

CC. *Space*: An area on a vessel or vessel section or within a shipyard such as, but not limited to: cargo tanks or holds; pump or engine rooms; storage lockers; tanks containing flammable or combustible liquids, gases, or solids; rooms within buildings; crawl spaces; tunnels; or accessways. The atmosphere within a space is the entire area within its bounds.

DD. *Upper Explosive Limit (UEL)*: The maximum concentration of flammable vapor in air above which propagation of flame does not occur on contact with a source of ignition.

EE. *Vessel*: Every description of watercraft or other artificial contrivance used, or capable of being used, as a means of transportation on the water, including special purpose floating structures not primarily designed for or used as a means of transportation on water.

FF. *Vessel Section*: A sub-assembly, module, or other component of a vessel being built, repaired, or broken.

GG. *Visual Inspection*: The physical survey of the space, its surroundings and contents to identify hazards such as, but not limited to, restricted accessibility, residues, unguarded machinery, and piping or electrical systems.

XII. Application. This instruction applies OSHA-wide to all interventions, inspections and violation abatement assistance related to confined and enclosed spaces and other dangerous atmospheres in shipyard employment. This instruction also applies to OSHA outreach efforts that include compliance assistance, cooperative programs, training, and education.

Further, this instruction applies to State Plan States (see paragraph VII.) and all State consultation programs with jurisdiction over employment activities at shipyards and boatyards. State consultation programs are expected to provide safety and health program assistance, training, education, hazard identification and abatement assistance to employers in shipyards and boatyards.

NOTE: Comprehensive guidance for OSHA offices to establish or support intervention and inspection programs in the shipyard employment industry, including 29 CFR Part 1915, Subpart B, is provided in OSHA Instruction CPL 02-00-142, the Shipyard Employment "Tool Bag" Directive, August 3, 2006.

XIII. Background. On November 29, 1988, OSHA published a proposed rule in the Federal Register (53 FR 48092) to revise OSHA standards for explosive and other dangerous atmospheres in shipyard employment on vessels and vessel sections, 29 CFR Part 1915, Subpart B. During the same time, the Shipyard Employment Standards Advisory Committee (SESAC) currently known as the Maritime Advisory Committee for Occupational Safety and Health (MACOSH), was established to provide OSHA with guidance in revising OSHA standards including 29 CFR Part 1915, Subpart B. On February 27, 1989, the record to the proposed rulemaking closed. OSHA received over 40 comments in response to the 29 CFR Part 1915, Subpart B proposal. However, the Agency received no requests to hold a hearing; therefore, no hearing was held.

On June 5, 1989, OSHA published a proposed rule for permit-required confined spaces in general industry (54 FR 24080). This proposed general industry standard for confined space entry (29 CFR 1910.146) was intended to apply to land-side operations within shipyards, including all operations and work areas such as fabricating shops, machine shops, and staging areas.

At the SESAC meeting on April 25-26, 1990, the Committee recommended that the scope of proposed 29 CFR Part 1915, Subpart B be expanded to include all confined and enclosed space operations within shipyard employment. Additionally, it was recommended that the title of the subpart be modified to include "other dangerous atmospheres." On June 24, 1992, OSHA published a notice reopening the record for Subpart B in order to obtain public comment on the land-side applicability of the standard and on six other issues. The comment period for this notice extended through September 22, 1992, and OSHA received 53 comments in response to the notice.

The final rule on the General Industry Permit-Required Confined Spaces standard, 29 CFR 1910.146, was published in the Federal Register on January 14, 1993 (58 FR 4462). Shipyards were omitted from the scope of this final general industry standard because the Agency determined that it was more appropriate to address this issue under 29 CFR Part 1915, Subpart B.

The final Confined and Enclosed Spaces and Other Dangerous Atmospheres in Shipyard Employment standard, 29 CFR Part 1915, Subpart B, was published in the Federal Register on July 25, 1994 (59 FR 37816), and became effective October 24, 1994.

A correction notice to this final rule was published in the Federal Register on March 16, 1995 (60 FR 14218), and became effective this same date. In addition to correcting several typographical errors, this notice made the following corrections to the final rule: clarified the order of testing before employees may enter a confined or enclosed spaces or other dangerous atmospheres; clarified when flammable atmospheres must be maintained above the upper explosive limit, such as during installation of ventilation or rescue; and clarified the limited locations and conditions where hot work may be performed without first being certified by a Marine Chemist.

Then on July 3, 2002, a technical amendment to 29 CFR Part 1915 was published in the Federal Register (67 FR 44533), and became effective this same date. With respect to Subpart B, this technical amendment corrected minor typographical, grammatical and other errors that were not substantive in nature, and did not impose additional compliance obligations on employers or reduce the protections provided to workers by these standards.

XIV. <u>29 CFR Part 1915, Subpart B, Standards Applicability and Guidance.</u>

    A.   <u>1915.11, Scope, Applicability and Definitions Applicable to Subpart B.</u> The scope and applicability of 29 CFR Part 1915, Subpart B (1915.11) covers shipyard employment on vessels, vessel sections, and land-side operations, regardless of geographic location. As discussed in the preamble to the standard (59 FR 37816), the entire Subpart B standard is applicable to all ship repair, shipbuilding, and shipbreaking operations, provided that the work is performed within OSHA's geographical jurisdiction (e.g., traditional shipyard or ship repair facility, vessel at anchor, vessel on sea trials, vessel in transit, all land-side operations within the physical boundaries of a shipyard, and inland shipyard employment which involves vessels or vessel sections). The only exception to the applicability of Subpart B standards within a shipyard is when activities are covered by the 29 CFR Part 1926, Construction Industry Standards, those activities are not subject to the provisions of 29 CFR Part 1915, Subpart B. Terms and definitions applicable to 29 CFR Part 1915, Subpart B are included at 1915.11(b). These Subpart B definitions, which were derived in large part from the National Fire Protection Association (NFPA) 306 standard, are provided to facilitate compliance with the 29 CFR Part 1915 standard.

        1.   The scope and application of the definitions "employer" and "employee" under 29 CFR 1915.4 are expanded in Subpart B by 1915.11(a). For Subpart B, the definitions "employer" and "employee" include all shipyard employment on vessels, vessel sections, and land-side operations.

        2.   The scope and application of Subpart B covers all shipyard employment including any and all production and manufacturing activities conducted within a shipyard facility.

            a.   Examples of 29 CFR Part 1915, Subpart B applicability that apply at a shipyard facility include:

                (i) Shipbuilding, ship repair, and shipbreaking,

                (ii) Fabrication, repair or refurbishment of equipment,

                (iii) Component or equipment manufacturing,

                (iv) Work performed within the shipyard facility by employees of a company under contract to the shipyard (e.g., painting contractor), and

                (v) Work performed within the shipyard facility by employees of a public utility which is not construction related (e.g., telephone, sewer, and steam companies).

                NOTE: OSHA would not issue citations to an employer whose

employees enter land-side spaces under the permit-required confined space standard, provided that the entry is in compliance with 29 CFR 1910.146 and does not involve hot work. For entry involving hot work, the employer is always required to comply with 29 CFR Part 1915, Subpart B.

If the workplace being inspected or the principle office of the employer is in the 3rd, 5th, 9th, or 11th Circuit, there is case law that may affect the applicability of 29 CFR Part 1915. For clarification regarding applicability case law contact the appropriate Regional Solicitor's Office.

b. Examples of work performed at a shipyard facility which is not under the scope of 29 CFR Part 1915, Subpart B include:

(i) Construction activities covered by 29 CFR Part 1926.

3. The scope and application of Subpart B covers all inland shipyard employment involving vessels or vessel sections.

a. Examples of 29 CFR Part 1915, Subpart B applicability that apply at an inland facility (not a shipyard facility) include:

(i) Vessel construction, repair or refurbishment,

(ii) Vessel section construction, repair or refurbishment, and

(iii) Manufacturing and fabrication of components and equipment for installation into vessels or vessel sections at the facility.

b. Examples of work performed at an inland facility (not a shipyard facility) which is not under the scope of 29 CFR Part 1915, Subpart B include:

(i) Manufacturing or fabrication of components and equipment for transport/shipment to another facility for installation into a vessel or vessel section (29 CFR Part 1910 applies), and

(ii) Repair or refurbishment of components and equipment (e.g., propellers, electronic components, ship service generators) (29 CFR Part 1910 applies).

4. The jurisdiction of OSHA over any vessel is limited to when the vessel is located within a jurisdiction covered by the Occupational Safety and Health Act of 1970 (see Section 4(a), 29 U.S.C. 653(a) of the OSH Act). OSHA may exercise authority over the working conditions of employees who are exposed to occupational hazards while working on vessels (i.e., inspected vessels, uninspected vessels, and uninspected commercial fishing industry vessels) or who are otherwise engaged in shipyard employment to the extent that the working conditions are not subject to

4(b)(1) preemption by another federal agency (see CPL 02-01-047, *OSHA Authority Over Vessels and Facilities on or Adjacent to U.S. Navigable Waters and the Outer Continental Shelf (OCS)*). For Federal civil service mariners (CIVMARs) see *Field Operations Manual, Chapter 10, Section III - Maritime*.

B. 1915.7, Competent Person. The following paragraphs summarize and discuss the principal requirements in effect for Part 1915, Subpart A, 1915.7.

1. The standard does not require employers to specifically use and maintain the Form OSHA 73, "Designation of Competent Person." Employers have the option of maintaining a written roster of designated employees or issuing a written statement that a Marine Chemist will always be used for the required inspections and tests (1915.7(b)(2)(i)). The employer also has the option of choosing the form or format of the written roster or statement. The roster of designated persons, or the use of a Marine Chemist statement, must be maintained at the place of employment or other location (e.g., main office of the employer), and such roster or statement must be made available to the Assistant Secretary of OSHA, Director of NIOSH, and employees and their representatives upon request (1915.7(b)(2)(ii)). When used, the roster must contain the following information as a minimum: employer's name, the designated competent person's name(s), and the date the employee was trained as a competent person (1915.7(b)(2)(iii)).

    a. It is emphasized that the employer is permitted to use any form or format of reporting that identifies the employer, the employees who are designated as competent persons, and the date such persons were trained. Alternatively, the employer must issue a written statement that a Marine Chemist will be used to perform all atmospheric testing. OSHA continues to recognize the Form OSHA 73 as an acceptable recordkeeping method, but does not require its specific use. (NOTE: Since the Form OSHA 73 is not specifically required, if used, it does not need to be provided to the OSHA area office each time a change is made.)

    b. There is no need to know when the roster or Form OSHA 73 was prepared, as long as the list of competent persons represents the current situation when it was created. However, it is important to record when a competent person was trained in order to confirm that he or she was trained as required at the time the inspection or testing was performed.

2. The standard does not require employers to specifically use and maintain the Form OSHA 74, "Log of Inspections and Tests by Competent Person." Employers must maintain a record of inspections and tests. However, the employer has the option of choosing the form or format. Such records must be posted in the immediate vicinity of the affected operations while work is in progress and be maintained for a period of at least three months from the completion date of the specific job for which they were generated

($1915.7(d)(2)$). The employer must make required inspection and testing records available for inspection by the Assistant Secretary of OSHA, Director of NIOSH, and employees and their representatives ($1915.7(d)(3)$).

3. The standard requires employers to ensure that the competent person, Marine Chemist or Certified Industrial Hygienist performing any tests in Subparts B, C, D, or H of Part 1915, records the following information for each test: location, date, time, inspected space(s) location, specific operations performed, test results, and any instructions ($1915.7(d)(1)$). OSHA recognizes the Form OSHA 74 as an acceptable record-keeping method, but does not require its specific use.

4. The standard requires that the employer designate at least one competent person for the purpose of testing work space atmospheres in shipyard employment, unless all of the employer's testing under Subpart B is performed by a Marine Chemist ($1915.7(b)(1)$). The following are noted with respect to compliance with this paragraph of Subpart B:

    a. A "Coast Guard Authorized Person" cannot be substituted for the "competent person" required by $1915.7(b)(1)$, because it has been determined that the training required for a Coast Guard Authorized Person does not provide all the skills and knowledge required of a competent person.

    b. Exception. An employer is allowed to designate any person, who meets the applicable portions of the criteria for a competent person per $1915.7(c)$, as a competent person who is limited to performing testing for the following specific situations:

        (i) Repair work on small craft in boatyards where only combustible gas indicator tests are required for fuel tank leaks or when using flammable paints below decks,

        (ii) Building of wooden vessels where only knowledge of the precautions to be taken when using flammable paints is required,

        (iii)The breaking of vessels where there is no fuel oil or other flammable hazard, and

        (iv) Tests and inspections performed to comply with $1915.35(b)(8)$ and $1915.36(a)(5)$. (NOTE: Both of these paragraphs involve the inspection of electrical power and lighting cables only).

5. Criteria for a Competent Person. The criterion of $1915.7(c)$ requires the competent person to have the skills and knowledge necessary to perform atmospheric testing. Because each shipyard is unique, how much training a competent person must have and how often it must be repeated is a responsibility of the employer. The employer is in the best position to determine what skills and knowledge must be reinforced and what

resource information needs to be presented. This performance-based approach allows the employer the necessary flexibility to determine what skills and knowledge must be reinforced and what resource information needs to be made available to the competent person for the unique conditions of each shipyard. The following comments and discussion are provided with respect to 1915.7(c):

a.   1915.7(c)(1) requires that the competent person be able to understand and carry out the written or oral instructions left by a Marine Chemist, Coast Guard Authorized Person or Certified Industrial Hygienist.

b.   1915.7(c)(2) requires competent persons to have knowledge of Subparts B, C, D and H of 29 CFR Part 1915.

c.   1915.7(c)(3) requires that competent persons have knowledge of the structure, location and designation of spaces (including land-side spaces) where work is done.

d.   1915.7(c)(4) requires competent persons to have the ability to use and interpret the readings of oxygen indicators, combustible gas indicators, and carbon dioxide indicators. Competent persons also must be able to calibrate all testing equipment used, and the equipment is not limited to those listed above. As technologies develop and new chemical hazards are encountered in shipyard employment, competent persons will use new types of environmental monitors and detectors. Skill in the use of this new equipment will be necessary for competent persons to be able to identify sources of hazardous exposures. In order for the competent person to have the ability to read and interpret the readings of any type of indicator, he or she must be familiar enough with the instrument to calibrate it.

e.   1915.7(c)(5) requires competent persons to have the ability to perform all required tests and inspections as set forth in Subparts B, C, D and H of 29 CFR Part 1915.

f.   1915.7(c)(6) requires competent persons to have the ability to evaluate spaces after a test to determine the need for further testing by a Marine Chemist or Certified Industrial Hygienist. This requirement makes it clear that there may be atmospheric conditions present in the shipyard that cannot be evaluated effectively by a person trained only to the competent person level, and that the competent person must be able to determine when more highly trained individuals are needed to properly and accurately evaluate an atmosphere.

g.   1915.7(c)(7) requires that a competent person must have the capability to maintain the records required by this section.

C.   <u>1915.12, Precautions and the Order of Testing Before Entering Confined and Enclosed Spaces and Other Dangerous Atmospheres</u>. The procedures and requirements for entering confined and enclosed spaces and other dangerous atmospheres in shipyard employment are unique to this industry. A "permit entry" system is not required by OSHA for the shipyard industry. Instead, Part 1915, Subpart B requires the use of specifically qualified individuals (such as Marine Chemists, Certified Industrial Hygienists (CIH), Competent Persons, and, in limited cases, Coast Guard Authorized Persons), and a system that contains evaluation mechanisms, tracking criteria, and control measures that are as protective as those of a 1910.146-type system.

      1.   The order of atmospheric testing to be conducted when determining hazards within confined and enclosed spaces and other dangerous atmospheres is: 1st-oxygen content, 2nd-flammability, and 3rd-toxicity.

      2.   The minimum level of oxygen for entry is 19.5% by volume, and testing is required for oxygen-enriched atmospheres (22.0% or higher).

      3.   It is specified when and under what conditions an employee may enter a space that has been found "Not Safe for Workers" or if oxygen-enriched "Not Safe for Workers - Not Safe for Hot Work."

      4.   The standard includes requirements that address: (a) training of all workers who enter spaces subject to 29 CFR Part 1915, Subpart B; (b) requirements for rescue teams; and (c) the exchange of hazard information between employers.

      5.   There is a requirement to visually inspect each space for other physical non-atmospheric hazards. Based on the visual inspection and other information available to the employer about non-atmospheric hazards, the employer may have to take specific action as delineated by other OSHA standards such as the following: electrical hazards (shipboard <u>1915.181</u>), piping system hazards (shipboard <u>1915.163</u>, land-side <u>1910.169</u> and <u>Subpart H</u>), and machinery hazards (shipboard <u>1915.164</u>, land-side <u>1910.212</u>).

         NOTE: "Shipboard" includes vessels and vessel sections.

      6.   A labeling requirement, "Not Safe for Workers - Not Safe for Hot Work," is required if concentrations are found to contain 10% or higher of LEL even when employees are permitted to enter for emergency purposes or for short durations to install ventilation (<u>29 CFR 1915.12(b)(3)</u>).

         NOTE: 29 CFR 1915.12(b)(3)(iii) states, "Atmospheres at or above the upper explosive limit are maintained." This does not suggest that flammable gases or vapors should be added to a space to maintain the UEL (upper explosive limit). Only atmospheres that are already at or above the UEL are to be maintained at those levels by minimizing dilution of the contaminates (e.g., close cross ventilation openings, do not begin ventilation, etc.) (see 29 CFR Part 1915, Subpart B preamble wording at

60 FR 14218).

7. In addition to a Marine Chemist or a Certified Industrial Hygienist, a "competent person" is permitted to initially inspect and test spaces for toxics, corrosives, and irritants; test results must show that toxics, corrosives and irritants are within the permissible exposure limits (PELs) and below IDLH levels before entry for physical inspection is permitted. Should the space be found not to contain toxic substances or contain quantities of toxic substances which can be made safe through the use of ventilation, then a "competent person" can authorize entry for employees. Otherwise, a Marine Chemist or a Certified Industrial Hygienist is required.

D. 1915.13, Cleaning and Other Cold Work. The procedures and requirements for cleaning and other cold work include:

1. The spaces that are covered by this paragraph are specified to facilitate the determination of applicability (1915.13(a)).

2. The requirement to take special care to prevent liquid residue spills into the water surrounding the vessel includes spills onto the surrounding work area (1915.13(b)(1)).

3. The requirement to test for and maintain flammable vapors below 10 percent of the LEL requires testing by a competent person to determine the concentration of flammable, combustible, toxic, corrosive, or irritant vapors (1915.13(b)(2)). Toxic, corrosive and irritant vapors are required to be maintained within the PELs and below IDLH levels (1915.13(b)(3)(ii)).

4. Ventilation is required to keep the concentration of flammable vapors below 10 percent of the LEL and within the PEL for the entire space (1915.13(b)(3)).

5. The standard requires testing to be conducted by the competent person as often as necessary during cleaning or cold work to ensure that air concentrations are below 10 percent of the LEL, within the PELs and below IDLH levels (1915.13(b)(4)).

6. The list of materials that must be cleaned up as work progresses includes corrosive and irritant materials (1915.13(b)(5)).

7. There are exceptions to the entry prohibition into spaces where the concentration of flammable or combustible vapors is 10 percent or more of the LEL (1915.13(b)(6)).

8. Ventilation exhaust vapor testing requires that all work be stopped if the competent person determines that concentrations of exhaust vapors which are hazardous to employees are accumulating (1915.13(b)(7) and (8)).

9. There is a requirement that signs prohibiting sources of ignition must be prominently posted (1915.13(b)(10)).

NOTE: For emergency spills or releases of hazardous substances, employers are required to comply with the requirements of 29 CFR 1910.120(q).

E. 1915.14, Hot Work. The procedures and requirements for hot work include:

1. A requirement to identify the locations and situations within shipyard employment where a Marine Chemist or Coast Guard Authorized Person is required to test/certify spaces "Safe for Hot Work" (1915.14(a)). The standard also identifies the locations and situations within shipyard employment where a competent person is permitted to visually inspect and test spaces "Safe for Hot Work" (1915.14(b)). A competent person is required to visually inspect and test spaces subject to 29 CFR Part 1915, Subpart B in which hot work is performed, except those spaces that specifically require a Marine Chemist or Coast Guard Authorized Person.

A Marine Chemist (for vessels, vessel sections, and shipyard employment land-side operations) or Coast Guard Authorized Person (for vessels and vessel sections) is required to test/certify all spaces and connected equipment (e.g., pipelines, heating coils, pumps, fittings) within, on, or immediately adjacent to spaces that contain or have contained combustible or flammable liquids or gases (e.g., cargo tanks, cargo tank manifolds and pipelines; or fuel tanks, fuel tank manifolds and pipelines) as "Safe for Hot Work."

2. There is an exception for dry cargo vessels, miscellaneous vessels, passenger vessels, and shipyard employment land-side operations that allows a competent person to visually inspect and test spaces that meet the standards for oxygen, flammability and toxicity in 1915.12, and are adjacent to spaces containing flammable gases or liquids, to be "Safe for Hot Work" as follows:

    a. When the adjacent space contains flammable liquids or gases, with a flash point above 150 degrees-Fahrenheit, then a competent person can visually inspect and test the space (1915.14(b)). However, hot work performed directly on the bulkhead of an adjacent space containing the flammable material must be tested/certified by a Marine Chemist (for vessels, vessel sections, and shipyard employment land-side operations) or a Coast Guard Authorized Person (for vessels and vessel sections). For hot work performed in the immediate proximity that may impact the bulkhead of such spaces, the competent person must ensure that measures are in place to shield the bulkhead of the space containing such flammables from hot work sparks, slag or heat.

    b. When the adjacent space contains flammable liquids or gases, with a flash point at or below 150 degrees-Fahrenheit, and the distance

15

between such spaces and the hot work is greater than 25 feet, then a competent person can visually inspect and test the space (if the hot work is 25 feet or closer to the adjacent space containing such flammables, then a Marine Chemist or Coast Guard Authorized Person is required to test/certify).

NOTE: Painting and related solvents, paint and preservative removers, and other vehicles capable of producing a flammable atmosphere, are covered by 29 CFR Part 1915, Subpart C, *Surface Preparation and Preservation*, and hot work shall not be performed until the paint, or other coating, is dry and all Subpart C requirements are met; entry into such spaces is addressed by 1915.12(a)(1). Welding, cutting and heating in way of preservative coatings (1915.53), and on drums, containers, or other structures that have contained flammable substances (1915.54), are covered by 29 CFR Part 1915, Subpart D, *Welding, Cutting and Heating*; entry into such spaces is addressed by 1915.12(a)(1). 29 CFR Part 1915, Subpart P, *Fire Protection in Shipyard Employment*, also contains provisions relating to hot work (such as requirements for fire watches).

F. 1915.15, Maintenance of Safe Conditions. The procedures and requirements for the maintenance of safe conditions include:

1. The scope and applicability of 1915.15 applies to all shipyard employment on vessels, vessel sections, and land-side operations.

2. Testing of atmospheres is required "as often as necessary" (1915.15(c) and (e)). The use of performance-based language for these testing requirements provides flexibility to competent persons in determining the time and need for testing atmospheres based on the conditions in each dangerous atmosphere. These conditions include: temperature, work in the tank, period of time elapsed, unattended tanks or spaces, work breaks, and ballasting or trimming (see Appendix A to 29 CFR Part 1915, Subpart B – *Compliance Assistance Guidelines for Confined and Enclosed Spaces and Other Dangerous Atmospheres*).

    NOTE: The shipyard employer must require the Marine Chemist or Coast Guard Authorized Person to record the atmospheric condition of each space. This is the only way that a competent person can compare his/her readings to those established by the Marine Chemist or Coast Guard Authorized Person, and confirm that there has been no change in the conditions of a space.

    EXAMPLE:
    PORT Cargo Tank, 20.9% 02, 0.0 LEL, < 0.5 ppm benzene.
    STBD Cargo Tank, 20.9% 02, 0.0 LEL, < 0.5 ppm benzene.
    FWD Deep Tank, 20.9% 02, 0.0 LEL, Toxics not performed.

3.   There is a requirement for the visual inspection of the space for conditions such as, but not limited to, tank leaks, pipeline leaks, build-up of hazardous substances, oily rags, insulation scraps, and combustible trash, as part of retesting and initial testing (1915.15(b), (c) and (e) and 1915.11(b) - definition for visual inspection).

4.   It is required that when changes occur that could alter conditions within the space or other dangerous atmospheres (such as local shifting of a vessel), work shall be stopped until the space is visually inspected, retested and found to comply with 1915.12, 1915.13, and 1915.14 (1915.15(b)).

     NOTE: Examples of changes that would warrant the stoppage of work include the opening of manholes or other closures, or the adjusting of a valve regulating the flow of hazardous materials.

G.   1915.16, Warning Signs and Labels. The scope and applicability of 1915.16 applies to all shipyard employment on vessels, vessel sections, and land-side operations. This section uses performance-based language. Specific posting requirements are addressed within their respective sections. Each sign/label posted must be presented in a manner that can be perceived and understood by all employees (1915.16(a)) (see "NOTE" below). An individual tank or other space need not be labeled separately if the whole area has been tested and all means of access to the area are labeled with the proper warning signs (1915.16(b)).

     NOTE: There are many methods such as dual language signs or pictorial graphics that an employer may use to ensure that employees can and do understand all warning signs and instructions addressing dangerous working conditions. This is consistent with the position OSHA has taken on other rulemakings that address signs, tags, and labels. For example, in 29 CFR 1910.145, OSHA permits the use of accident prevention tags using graphic or second language text (such as Spanish) where necessary. Moreover, the obligation to present signs and labels in a manner that can be perceived by all employees also means that the label or sign must be posted in a place where it will be effective. Other factors the employer must consider are size, material, and methods of attachment. In short, this performance-based language requires employers to provide adequate notice to all employees of dangerous working conditions, but leaves the method of presentation up to the employer.

H.   Appendix A to 29 CFR Part 1915, Subpart B. This appendix is a non-mandatory set of guidelines to assist employers and employees in complying with the requirements of 29 CFR Part 1915, Subpart B. The appendix provides explanatory information and educational material in order to facilitate the understanding of, and compliance with, the standard.

I.   Part 1915, Subpart B Flowcharts. In order to clarify the logical process for
        determining compliance with 29 CFR Part 1915, Subpart B requirements, six
        flowcharts have been developed and are provided in Appendix A to this
        instruction as follows:

        1.   Part 1915, Subpart B Flowchart – Sheet #1: Documentation and Training.

        2.   Part 1915, Subpart B Flowchart – Sheet #2: Precautions Before Entering.

        3.   Part 1915, Subpart B Flowchart – Sheet #3: Combustible/Flammable
                Checks.

        4.   Part 1915, Subpart B Flowchart – Sheet #4: Cold Work Checks.

        5.   Part 1915, Subpart B Flowchart – Sheet #5: Hot Work Checks.

        6.   Part 1915, Subpart B Flowchart – Sheet #6: Maintenance of Safe
                Conditions.

XV.   Coordination. This instruction will be coordinated by the Directorate of Enforcement
        Programs (DEP). Questions and comments should be directed to the Office of Maritime
        Enforcement (OME) at 202-693-2399.

APPENDIX A

PART 1915 SUBPART B FLOWCHART — SHEET #1: DOCUMENTATION AND TRAINING

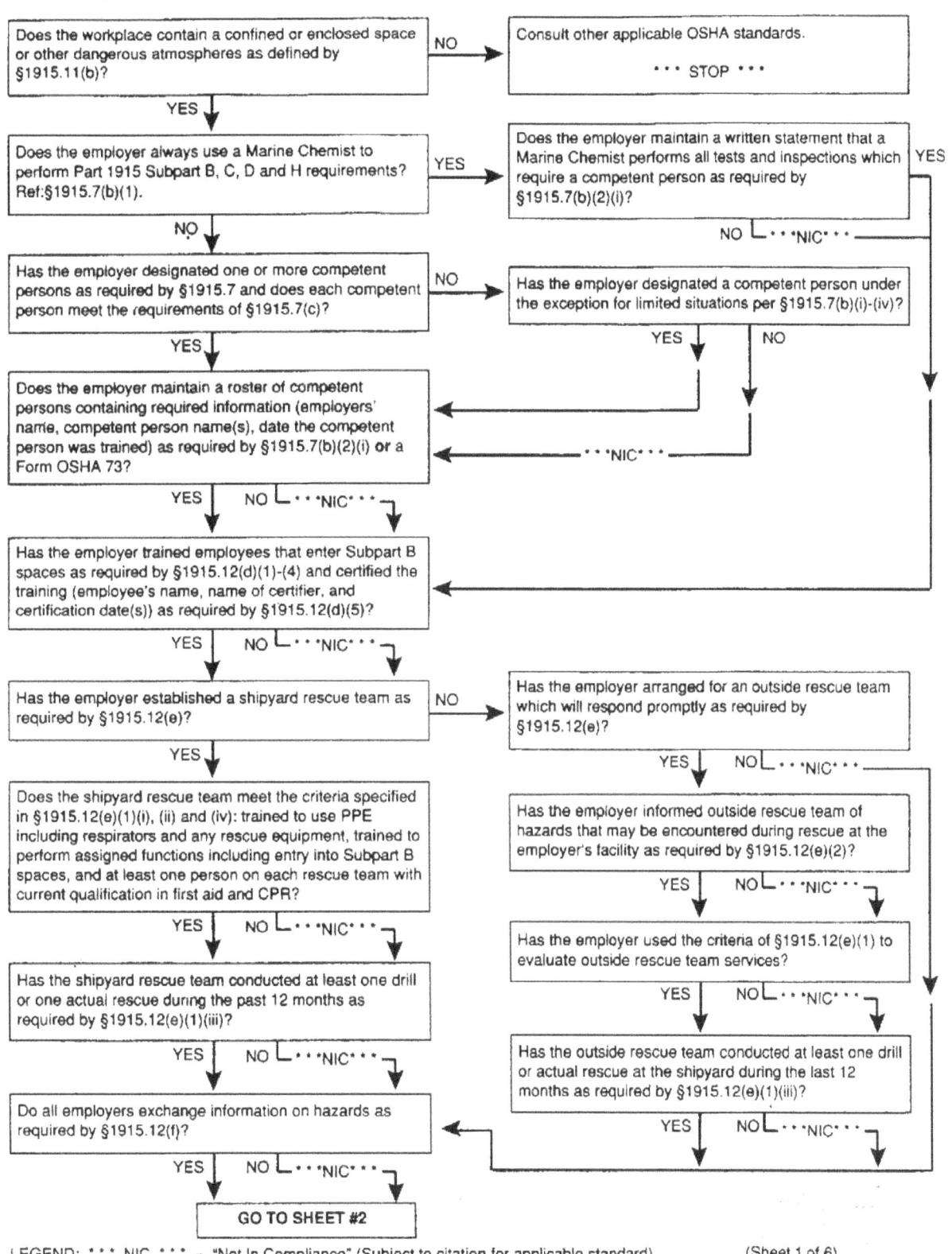

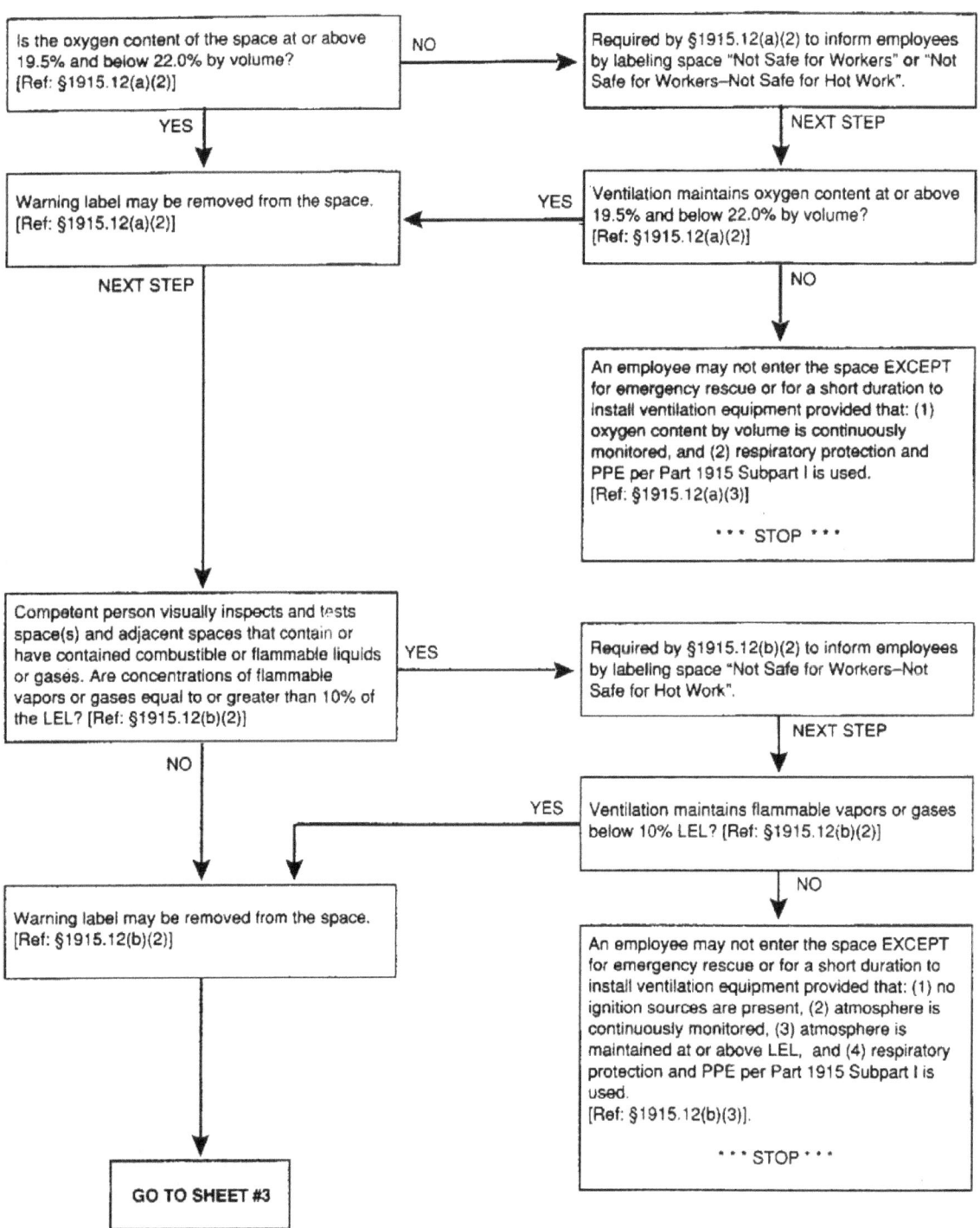

LEGEND: * * * NIC * * * = "Not In Compliance" (Subject to citation for applicable standard)

(Sheet 2 of 6)

PART 1915 SUBPART B FLOWCHART — SHEET #3: COMBUSTIBLE/FLAMMABLE CHECKS

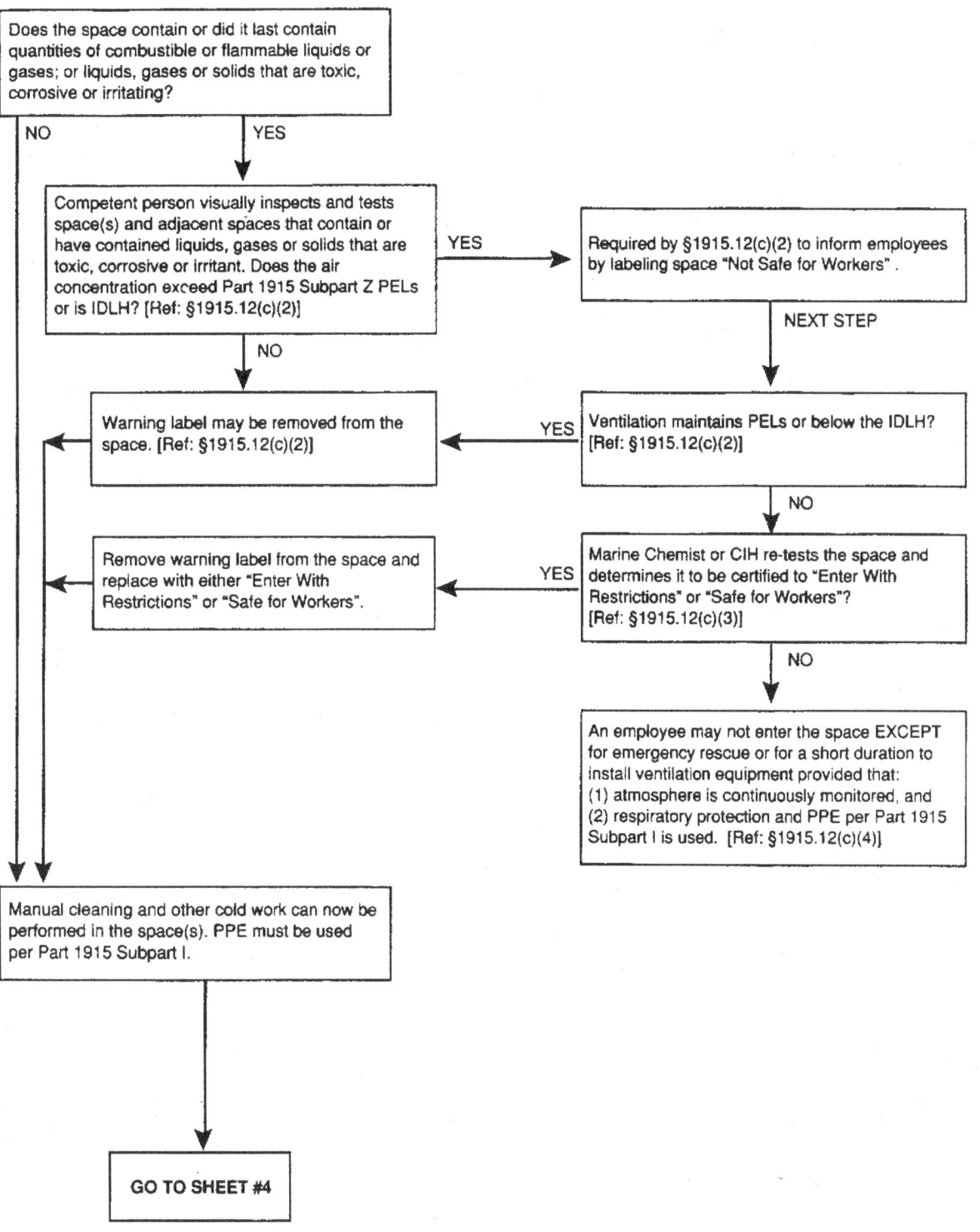

LEGEND: * * * NIC * * * = "Not In Compliance" (Subject to citation for applicable standard)

(Sheet 3 of 6)

PART 1915 SUBPART B FLOWCHART — SHEET #4: COLD WORK CHECKS

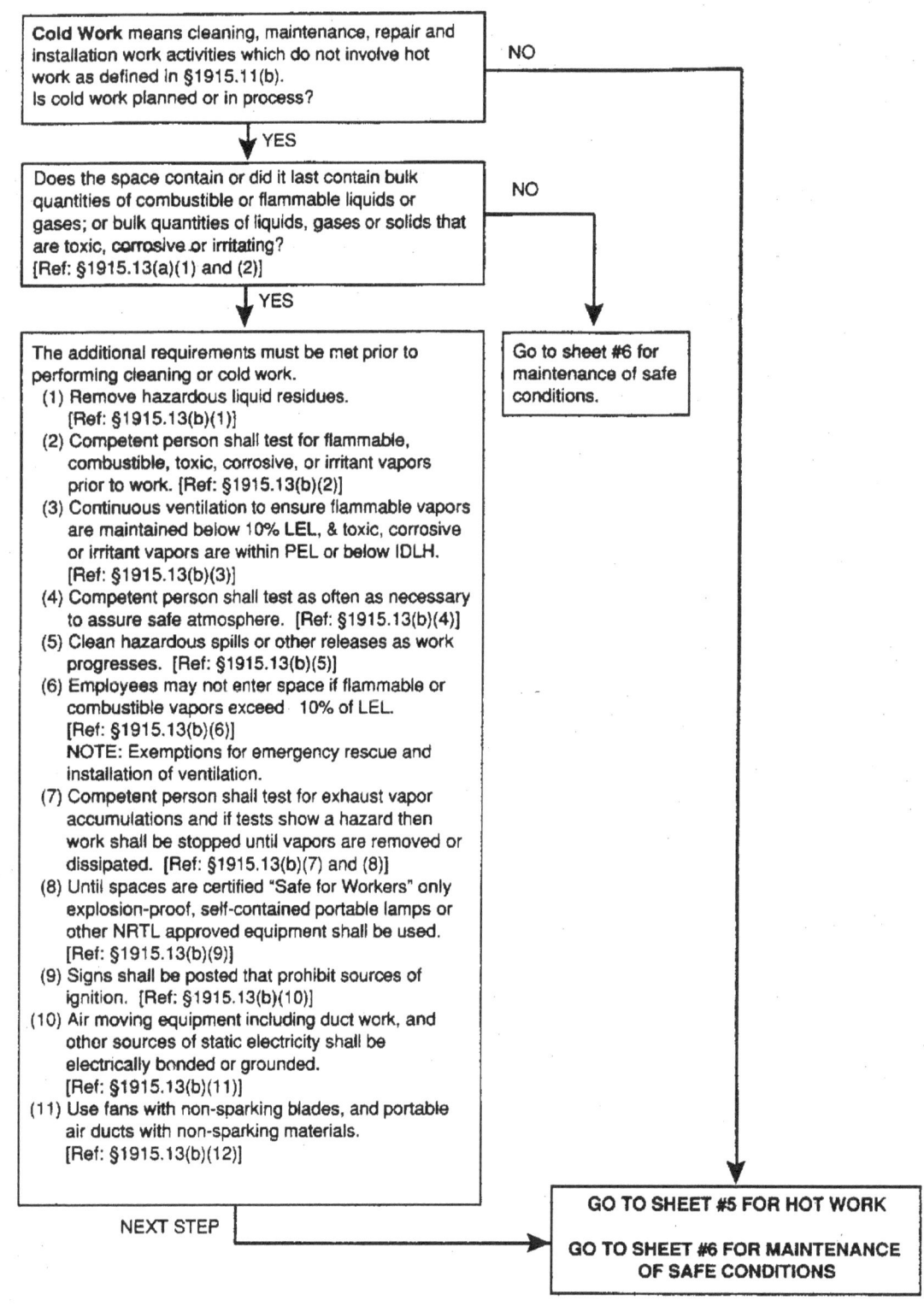

Cold Work means cleaning, maintenance, repair and installation work activities which do not involve hot work as defined in §1915.11(b).
Is cold work planned or in process?

→ NO

↓ YES

Does the space contain or did it last contain bulk quantities of combustible or flammable liquids or gases; or bulk quantities of liquids, gases or solids that are toxic, corrosive or irritating?
[Ref: §1915.13(a)(1) and (2)]

→ NO

↓ YES

Go to sheet #6 for maintenance of safe conditions.

The additional requirements must be met prior to performing cleaning or cold work.
(1) Remove hazardous liquid residues.
   [Ref: §1915.13(b)(1)]
(2) Competent person shall test for flammable, combustible, toxic, corrosive, or irritant vapors prior to work. [Ref: §1915.13(b)(2)]
(3) Continuous ventilation to ensure flammable vapors are maintained below 10% LEL, & toxic, corrosive or irritant vapors are within PEL or below IDLH. [Ref: §1915.13(b)(3)]
(4) Competent person shall test as often as necessary to assure safe atmosphere. [Ref: §1915.13(b)(4)]
(5) Clean hazardous spills or other releases as work progresses. [Ref: §1915.13(b)(5)]
(6) Employees may not enter space if flammable or combustible vapors exceed 10% of LEL.
   [Ref: §1915.13(b)(6)]
   NOTE: Exemptions for emergency rescue and installation of ventilation.
(7) Competent person shall test for exhaust vapor accumulations and if tests show a hazard then work shall be stopped until vapors are removed or dissipated. [Ref: §1915.13(b)(7) and (8)]
(8) Until spaces are certified "Safe for Workers" only explosion-proof, self-contained portable lamps or other NRTL approved equipment shall be used.
   [Ref: §1915.13(b)(9)]
(9) Signs shall be posted that prohibit sources of ignition. [Ref: §1915.13(b)(10)]
(10) Air moving equipment including duct work, and other sources of static electricity shall be electrically bonded or grounded.
   [Ref: §1915.13(b)(11)]
(11) Use fans with non-sparking blades, and portable air ducts with non-sparking materials.
   [Ref: §1915.13(b)(12)]

NEXT STEP →

GO TO SHEET #5 FOR HOT WORK

GO TO SHEET #6 FOR MAINTENANCE OF SAFE CONDITIONS

LEGEND: * * * NIC * * * = "Not In Compliance" (Subject to citation for applicable standard)

(Sheet 4 of 6)

A-4

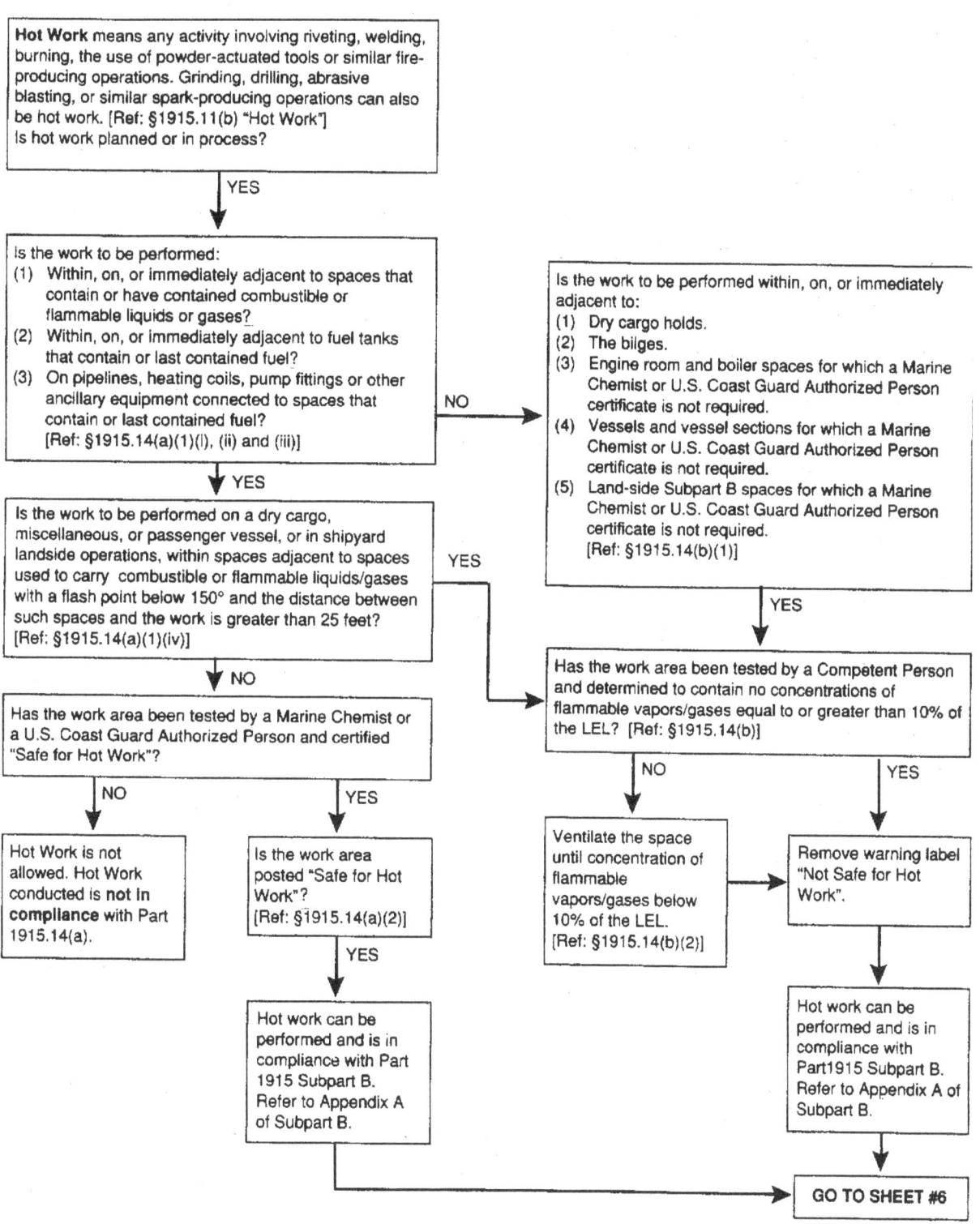

Hot Work means any activity involving riveting, welding, burning, the use of powder-actuated tools or similar fire-producing operations. Grinding, drilling, abrasive blasting, or similar spark-producing operations can also be hot work. [Ref: §1915.11(b) "Hot Work"]
Is hot work planned or in process?

↓ YES

Is the work to be performed:
(1) Within, on, or immediately adjacent to spaces that contain or have contained combustible or flammable liquids or gases?
(2) Within, on, or immediately adjacent to fuel tanks that contain or last contained fuel?
(3) On pipelines, heating coils, pump fittings or other ancillary equipment connected to spaces that contain or last contained fuel?
[Ref: §1915.14(a)(1)(l), (ii) and (iii)]

→ NO →

Is the work to be performed within, on, or immediately adjacent to:
(1) Dry cargo holds.
(2) The bilges.
(3) Engine room and boiler spaces for which a Marine Chemist or U.S. Coast Guard Authorized Person certificate is not required.
(4) Vessels and vessel sections for which a Marine Chemist or U.S. Coast Guard Authorized Person certificate is not required.
(5) Land-side Subpart B spaces for which a Marine Chemist or U.S. Coast Guard Authorized Person certificate is not required.
[Ref: §1915.14(b)(1)]

↓ YES

↓ YES

Is the work to be performed on a dry cargo, miscellaneous, or passenger vessel, or in shipyard landside operations, within spaces adjacent to spaces used to carry combustible or flammable liquids/gases with a flash point below 150° and the distance between such spaces and the work is greater than 25 feet?
[Ref: §1915.14(a)(1)(iv)]

→ YES →

Has the work area been tested by a Competent Person and determined to contain no concentrations of flammable vapors/gases equal to or greater than 10% of the LEL? [Ref: §1915.14(b)]

↓ NO

Has the work area been tested by a Marine Chemist or a U.S. Coast Guard Authorized Person and certified "Safe for Hot Work"?

↓ NO   ↓ YES

↓ NO   ↓ YES

Hot Work is not allowed. Hot Work conducted is **not in compliance** with Part 1915.14(a).

Is the work area posted "Safe for Hot Work"?
[Ref: §1915.14(a)(2)]

↓ YES

Ventilate the space until concentration of flammable vapors/gases below 10% of the LEL.
[Ref: §1915.14(b)(2)]

→

Remove warning label "Not Safe for Hot Work".

Hot work can be performed and is in compliance with Part 1915 Subpart B. Refer to Appendix A of Subpart B.

Hot work can be performed and is in compliance with Part1915 Subpart B. Refer to Appendix A of Subpart B.

↓

→ **GO TO SHEET #6**

LEGEND: * * * NIC * * * = "Not In Compliance" (Subject to citation for applicable standard)

(Sheet 5 of 6)

A-5

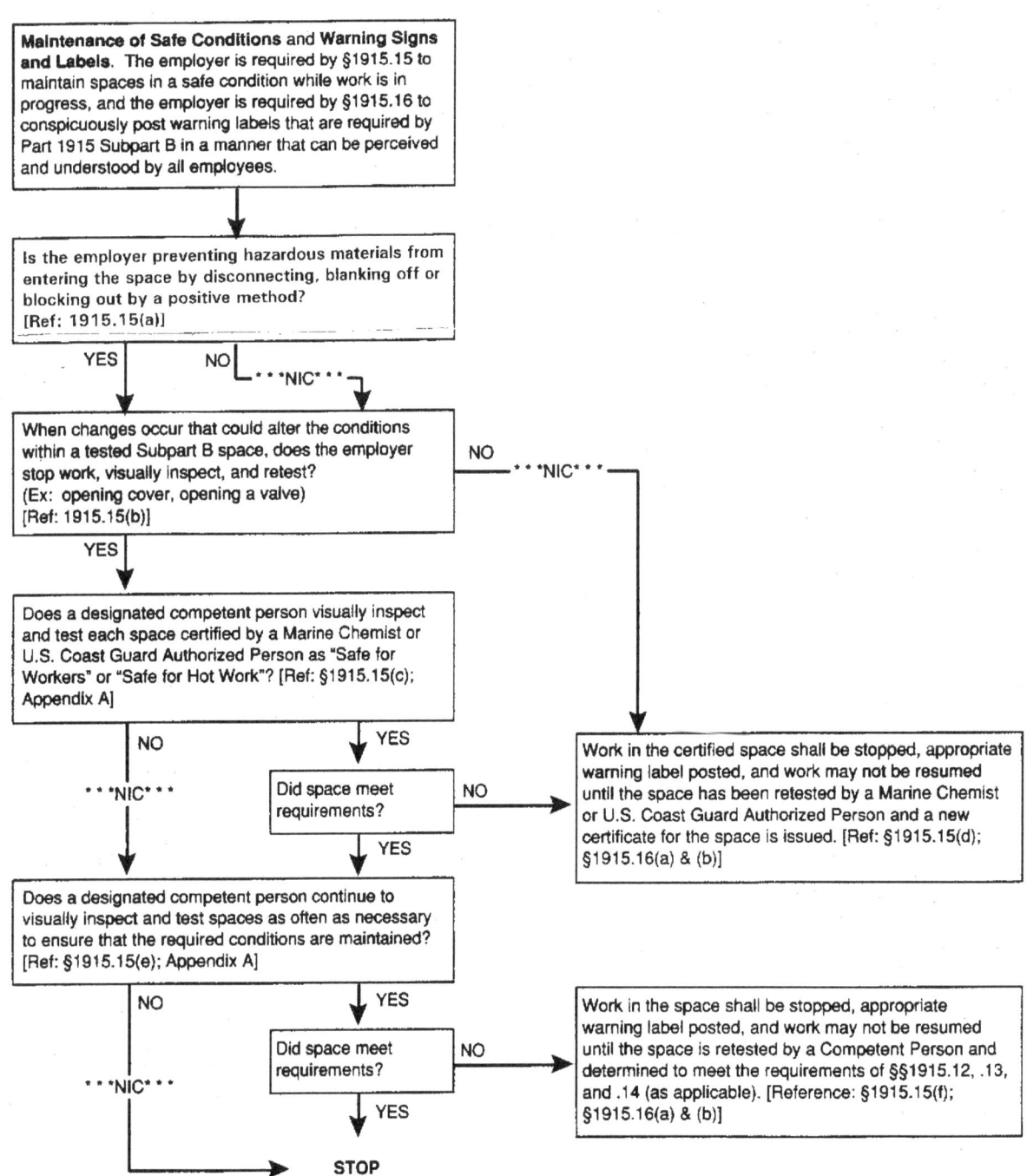

LEGEND: * * * NIC * * * = "Not In Compliance" (Subject to citation for applicable standard)